120 Quotes that will make you action-oriented

KNOW WHAT YOU KNOW

AF658271

GANESAN S. IYER

KNOW WHAT YOU KNOW
Ganesan S. Iyer

Published by Qurate Books Pvt. Ltd.

Published in 2023

ISBN: 978-93-58980-53-0

qurate
qauratebooks.com

Qurate Books Pvt. Ltd.
Goa 403523, India
www.quratebooks.com
Tel: 1800-210-6527, Email: info@quratebooks.com

The Praise for the Book

I am delighted to have, read the book insightful, stimulating practical tips to be applied for self & business development.

Dr. Dileep Mane,
Managing Director, Noble Hospitals,
Pune, Maharashtra.

This book is a must read outstanding!

Through his unique style Mr. Ganesan Iyer talks to the readers in a language that is very easy to understand.

While going through some of the quotes we feel the author is actually writing about us, his quotes are useful for personal & professional development.

Adway Rajhans,
Marketing manager,
Eisen pharmaceuticals co Pvt ltd, Pune, Maharashtra.

All the quotes in this book are in simple language, easy to understand, motivating, inspiring & encouraging, very useful for self & professional development.

Dhirendra Kumar,
Chief manager, Bank of India,
Pune, Maharashtra.

All the quotes in this book denote that simple things are ignored the most. Iyers list of quotes will help to get those on track.

Ankur Joshi,
CEO marketing,
Eisen Pharmaceuticals co Pvt ltd, Pune, Maharashtra.

Preface

I was born in Chennai & brought up in Mumbai, Maharashtra, India. I finished my science graduation, started a career in pharma field with PFIZER & after 11 years of service I started my own pharma company in Pune, Maharashtra, India ran successfully for 30 years. Since age was catching up no one to continue I closed the company. Later I started coaching, training & consulting for different types of organizations, colleges, hospitals, pharma companies, retailers & chemists association for the last 18 years & continuing. I am 79 years old.

I started reading, read almost 900 books till today from 2005 to 2023 almost 40 different subjects like attitude, behavior, communication, presentation skills, time management, stress management, teambuilding, selling, decision making, negotiation, conflict management, collaboration, human relationship, change, mind management, leadership, empathy & problem solving.

This triggered a desire in me to write a book to help people develop self & be benefitted in various aspects of life. I want to be a contributor to the society. I realized the importance of reading which helped me to develop myself but also added confidence & increased my courage for handling any situation.

Instead of writing a specific subject I thought I would convey my ideas in the form of quotes with in depth meaning, practical, which is easy to read, understand & apply on a daily basis to be benefitted for self development & professional development.

Two more books to follow with more quotes.

Good luck with best wishes

Ganesan S. Iyer

Preface

Introduction

I had mentioned that I would convey my ideas in the form of quotes because in my experience for the last so many years quotes though brief convey great meanings, useful in a daily walk of life. Easy to read, consumes minimum time, easy to understand & apply.

If anyone develops a habit of reading daily 5 quotes & tries to apply in suitable walks of life he will experience new learning.

These are self created quotes based on knowledge acquired, experience, interaction with different types of people & self creativity. It is in simple language, easy to apply in many situations almost daily & experience the difference.

Quotes will not only educate, but also add knowledge, confidence, courage, & improve vocabulary. Quotes are very factual, logical, day to day common experiences, meaningful, will improve analytical skills & they teach many things to develop self.

Each quote will be an eye opener, motivator & an encourager. So if any one wants to improve in all walks of life make it a point to read on a daily basis & apply. **Finally the sole intention of writing this book is to help as many people in the world to develop themselves, become better human beings & lead a happy life.**

Goodluck with best wishes

Ganesan S. Iyer

Mind
is a congested
junction

Ego makes you deaf

Don’t live with a doubt, seek clarification

Fear is
caused by, negative
imagination

One who looks for solution, solves the problems faster

Same actions
will not
produce different
results

When you are not attentive,
you are as good as absent

If you think you know everything you will not learn

Self awareness
saves you, from
many mistakes

Don't see everything through a narrow angle

Don’t regret,
a lost opportunity

Doing is
more important
than saying

Strong belief
brings confidence

Criticism without suggestion, is useless

Health is
the most
important asset

Your value increases, when promises are honored

Clarity will
help you,
understand faster

Adaptability
makes you stable
& stronger

Self control
is the most
difficult thing

Gossiping
is the biggest
waste of time

Inaction is the root cause of failure

Never start any venture with doubt

Educating someone is the best charity

Preconception misleads you

Exploiting the helpless,
is the biggest sin

Different opinions
help us,
with more options

Be motivated
by ambition
not by fear

Attitude makes every difference

Fear is the worst killer

By Reading you come to know many things

Most difficult change is to change the habit

When ever you are
alone your best
company is
your own mind

You can't learn from a man who agrees to every thing you say

Listening shows respect & willingness to know other's opinion

Difficult situation sharpens your thinking

Overconfidence
is as bad as lack
of confidence

Assurance is not a guarantee

Irritated mind
cannot focus

Don't pretend deaf when people point out your mistake

Behavior can't be forced

Motivated people are fresh & active

Managing by threatening is poor management

Distraction causes low productivity

Associate with whom, you can learn

Curious people ask more questions

Faith increases confidence, fear decreases confidence

Impressions and facts don't match

You can't listen,
when disinterested

Control over
tongue keeps
conflicts away

"Understanding keeps, relation intact"

Don't hate when people differ, be curious to know why

Have the courage to say no than avoiding

Problems unsolved, do not disappear

Appreciation at appropriate time increases the yield

Seek feedback
to improve

Don't blame destiny, when something goes wrong

Difference of opinion does not mean enmity

You can't buy affection

Self-made barriers stop your progress

Adamancy is responsible for non cooperation

You can't grow,
without a mistake

Anger is an enemy

It is very difficult to erase the feelings of dislike

Endless discussion,
leads to indecision

Hatred & dislike, consumes energy

Smile makes you attractive & easily acceptable

Growth has
no limit

Family is your biggest strength

Anxiety is self-created

Perception &
interpretation
makes the
difference

Treat criticism, as constructive suggestion

You are judged by performance & not by impression

Remaining cool
in tough situations,
is an advantage

You require courage to say I was wrong

When confused keep quiet

Motivation requires a reason

Easiest way to
fail is to stop
making effort

Respecting others does not, reduce your value

Never say no,
to an opportunity

Don't ignore a negative feedback

“Never stop learning & growing”

Disappointment is because you want everything your way

Every day is a different day

Every action has a consequence

Don't allow petty differences to spoil the relationship

Mannerism creates a good image

Finding Solution is better, than complaining

Happiness originates from home

Keep a hobby for diversion

Risk & courage
are part of success

Start the day
with motivating
activity

You will have
nothing to hide,
if you tell
the truth

While listening, focus exclusively on the speaker

Procrastination results in loss

Courage and confidence are twins for problem solving

Everyone has strength & weakness accept them

Take the initiative to repair the disturbed relationship

Action is best remedy to counter fear

Attention improves observation

Behavior changes,
only when
purpose changes

Never depend
on others to
motivate you

Pending issues keep you nagging

Comfortable life
does not
come easy

Ego is an inflated image

You cannot
lead life
without sacrifice

Never postpone health issues

Desire is the starting point for achieving anything in life

Occupied mind
has no
time to worry

Don’t comment on others without knowing the truth

Excuse is an escape route

Multitasking consumes more time & energy

It is better to face the problem than to worry in advance

Growth cannot take place without risk and change

Wherever emotion is involved decision is difficult

Reversing the decision is better than suffering the consequences

Never challenge
self respect

If you want
to be different
don't copy

Believe in reciprocating

Don't regret your mistake find a way to rectify

Good listeners are liked by everyone

ABOUT THE AUTHOR

Ganesan S. Iyer

The author stays in Pune Maharashtra India.
He is a Science graduate. Has a rich experience of pharma, owned a pharma company for 30 years. Doing coaching, training & consulting since last 18 years for different types of organizations, in various subjects. He has read about 900 books of different subjects. He is 79 years old. He is a powerful speaker.